AuthorHouse™
1663 Liberty Drive
Bloomington, IN 47403
www.authorhouse.com
Phone: 1 (800) 839-8640

Published by AuthorHouse 09/25/2018

ISBN: 978-1-5462-6123-0 (sc)
978-1-5462-6124-7 (e)

Library of Congress Control Number: 2018911366

Print information available on the last page.

This book is printed on acid-free paper.

For the Love of Pink and Blue

By Alina Jemerson & The Twins

Illustrated By Jonathan Craig

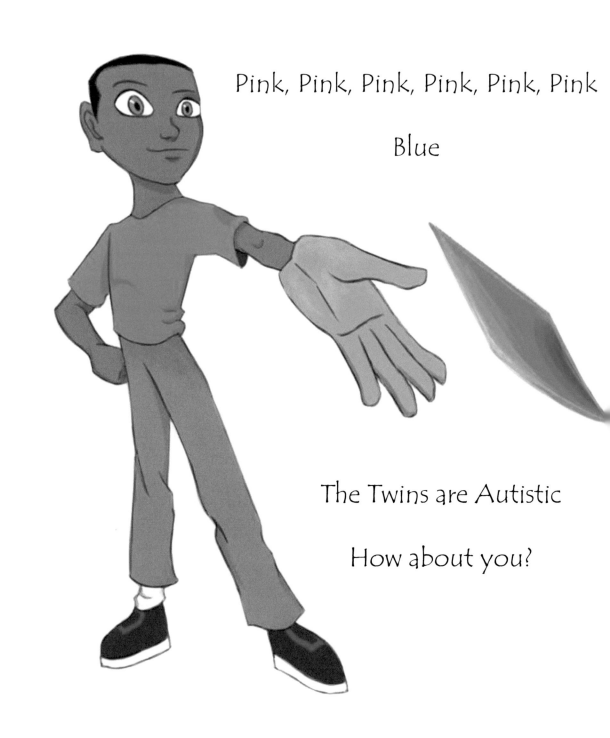

Pink, Pink, Pink, Pink, Pink, Pink

Blue

The Twins are Autistic

How about you?

This is Amora!

She is a Twin.

This is her brother Junior!

His voice lies within.

Amora does most of the talking and Junior hums along.

They sound
pretty good
when they
sing songs.

The Twins can be really silly.

They can be really sad.

They always
take turns
making
mommy mad.

So many feelings can happen in one day.

It can always seem so cloudy and grey.

But when
it comes
down to Pink
and Blue.

Amora and Junior will always push through.

Amora has her Doll that wears a Pink Dress.

That Doll brings her comfort but she's a real mess.

Junior does love
the Color Blue,

But a Phone

or a Tablet will do.

After the excitement has all come down,

It's time to eat and The Twins don't fool around.

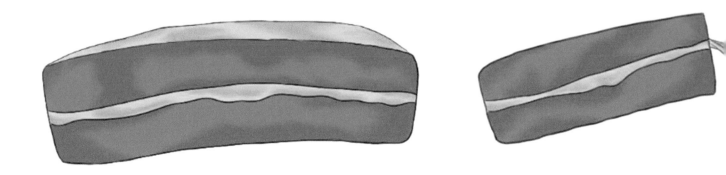

Breakfast, lunch, and dinner

Dinner, lunch and breakfast

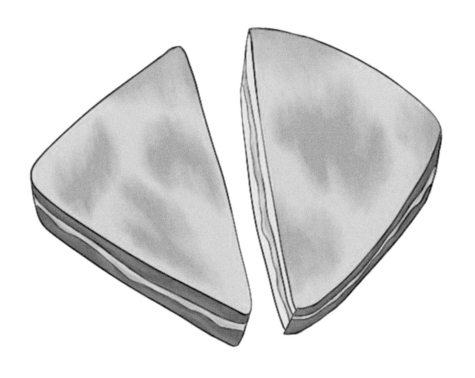

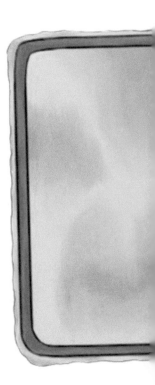

For some reason they
only eat grilled
cheese sandwhiches.

But Autism
Parents know

Maybe
pancakes
every now
and then.

that French
fries are the
real best
friend.

When it's all said
and done, The Twins
are no different
from You and I.

They are filled
with love
and good
Lullabies.

There is always Pink.
There is always Blue.

Sometimes Grey
is in there too.

Amora and Junior can't tell when they are not careful.

IT really
doesn't matter
because it's
the Love that
truly makes
them special.

Printed in the United States
By Bookmasters